Launching your aviation career

Published by 107 School LLC,
June 4, 2024

Do you love to learn?
Enjoy flying or travel?
Looking for a new career?

Published by 107 School LLC,
April 20, 2024
© 2024 107 School LLC

The main source of the information presented within this publication is the FAA and their publications. This information is presented for the benefit of the audience. Dilligence on the part of the reader is assumed as the information may change.

107 School makes no warranties based on the use of this information, it is intended to educate prospective pilots. You can find 107 School online at www.107school.com
Version 1.1
06/01/2024

This book brought to you by 107 School

107 School offers a Part 107 training course. We believe flying small unmanned aircraft is the logical place to start your aviation career. It's an affordable and accessible starting point for future aviators, and a good introduction to the processes and procedures of the FAA and dealing with them. You can check out our course online at www.107school.com to learn more.

*Are you interested in flying?
Looking for a great career?
Want more than a job?*

How to start your aviation career

Do you have an interest in aviation? Are you thinking about a career?

There are plenty to chose from: you could be a pilot flying anything from a drone to an airship, or you could be in the control tower helping pilots find their way -- or even be the person who designs and builds aircraft. You could even design, build or manage an airport.

The purpose of this book is to show you some of the careers out there -- and provide you with insight into the training process and the different paths you can take to get there.

It is meant for both people considering a career in aviation, and anyone considering including aviation in their career. It's a great reference for anyone starting the journey towards working in aviation. There are an incredible number of career paths in aviation.

Your Part 107 can be the first step

107 School recommends earning your remote pilot certificate to launch your aviation career journey. It's why 107 School offers a Part 107 training course. After a decade producing courses from everything from Remote Pilot through Certificated Flight Instructor, starting with a course on flying small unmanned aircraft was the logical place to start, and it's a logical place for future manned pilots to start as well.

AUTHOR:
MEG GODLEWSKI

Meg Godlewski is an aviation journalist with more than 20 years experience as a flight instructor.

Godlewski has been recognized as a Gold Seal instructor by the FAA and as a Master instructor from both the National Association of Flight Instructors (NAFI) and the Society of Aviation and Flight Educators (SAFE).

She writes for multiple aviation publications including Flying Magazine, and is an expert in creating scenario based simulator training.

Becoming a Pilot

BY MEG GODLEWSKI

Let's begin with how to become a pilot. It's likely the first career you think of in aviation, and it's a pretty important one, and there is a big need for more pilots. And since you can pilot anything from a small unmanned aircraft to a hot air balloon, helicopter, or airplane, there are a lot of types of pilots.

No matter what you want to fly, your training will be a combination of ground study known as Ground School where you learn about aeronautical subjects and Flight Training where you learn how to control the aircraft.

Ground School

In Ground School you learn about rules and regulations, the aircraft systems, aerodynamics, navigation, weather, aircraft procedures, emergency procedures, human factors, and airspace.

This knowledge will be applicable to every certificate you earn from Remote Pilot which allows you to fly a small Unmanned Aerial Vehicle also known as a drone, all the way up to Airline Transport Pilot which makes you eligible to fly for an airline.

Each ground school is specialized to the certificate (license) you seek. The Federal Aviation Administration tests students on the training these courses offer to make sure you have the knowledge you need and are prepared to fly the aircraft in the federal airspace system.

Ground School is often taught by a Certificated Flight Instructor (CFI) who has a certificate from the Federal Aviation Administration that permits them to teach both in the air and on the ground, or by a FAA certified Ground Instructor who are qualified teach ground schools, provided their certificate is for the material to be taught.

An Advanced Ground Instructor (AGI) can teach ground school for commercial pilot candidates in addition to private and sport pilot candidates a Basic Ground Instructor can teach, and an Instrument Ground Instructor can teach instrument rating candidates.

In addition to teaching people how to fly, I teach ground schools and
also provide training in Advanced Aviation Training Devices (AATDs or
simulators). Ground school is the most important link in the chain.

Ground school can be taught face to face in a conventional classroom, or you can opt for an online course that allows you to study and learn at your own pace, like 107 School's online ground school for your part 107 ground training.

The official FAA knowledge exams are offered by a third party company, and you pay for every attempt. The Part 107 exam currently costs $175 per attempt, that's why it's important to study for the exam.

No matter which route you choose, be sure to take notes during the lessons. If there is something that confuses you, and you are working with a flight or ground instructor, ask for clarification, or look up the material yourself in an FAA-approved text.

FAA Publications

Federal Aviation Regulations/Aeronautical Information Manual (FARAIM)

Federal Aviation Regulations:
https://www.faa.gov/regulations_policies/faa_regulations

Aeronautical Information Manual:
https://www.faa.gov/air_traffic/publications/atpubs/aim_html/index.html

Pilot's Handbook of Aeronautical Knowledge
https://www.faa.gov/regulations_policies/handbooks_manuals/aviation/phak

Airplane Flying Handbook
https://www.faa.gov/regulations_policies/handbooks_manuals/aviation/airplane_handbook

There is so much knowledge required to be a pilot no one can remember all of it, so we rely on the ability to looking things up in FAA approved sources. The FAA is our regulating authority, and their word is gospel. This is a partial list. Hard copies are available on paper through pilot supply stores or Amazon, or they can be downloaded from the FAA

Knowledge Tests

After you complete ground school and have passed the course, you will be issued an endorsement that will allow you to take the knowledge test. This is done by appointment at an FAA-approved Knowledge Testing Center.

You can go online to find one closest to you. They are often located at flight schools at airports.

Pro-tip: These tests are are sometimes called "the written test" because back in the old days you used a pencil and paper to answer the questions. These days everything is done on computer, but pilots often refer to it as the written.

Before the Knowledge Test

Before you make an appointment to take any FAA test you need to obtain an Federal Tracking Number known as an FTN. This is created by the FAA's Integrated Airman Certification and Rating Application profile, commonly referred to as IACRA which is a website portal the FAA maintains, prior to registering for a knowledge test.

A CFI can help you fill out the online application, or you can follow the available instructions.

You will need to have a user name and password — most people use their email address for a username. Write this down and keep it someplace secure.

This FTN will be with you for the rest of your life and will be referenced every time you add a pilot certificate or rating. After you complete your remote pilot certificate you can move ahead to private pilot's certificate, earn an instrument rating, then your commercial certificate, flight instructor certification, and Airline Transport rating if you'd like to become an airline pilot.

You will need to bring a valid government-issued photo ID with you to the testing center.

Pro-tip: before you go to the testing center take several practice tests online. You can do a search to find them. Don't go into the testing center for the real test until you are scoring in the 90s, because most people lose 10 points when they walk in the door. Aviation tests are not ones you want squeak through.

For those of you considering a Part 107 remote pilot's certificate 107 School has several full videos devoted to these topics, we will show you how to navigate the entire process, easily.

40 hours isn't realistic

Real world tip: The regulations for pilot training were written decades ago when we didn't have the complicated airspace, radios or busy lives that we have today.

Most private pilots have an average of 60 to 70 hours of training before they take their flight tests which are known as check rides.

Flight School

Flight school is where you learn to fly the aircraft.

There are two kinds of flight schools: Part 141 and Part 61, named for the section of law they are operated under.

Part 141 is the more structured of the two.

Part 141 is often used by aviation colleges and academies. There is a syllabus that is strictly followed. You are limited to specific airports you can fly to for training flights, and there may be rules prohibiting doing any flights outside the 141 program.

Under Part 141 an applicant can qualify with as little as 35 hours of flight experience for their Private Pilot certificate which is the first aviation certificate earned on the path towards flying manned aircraft professionally.

Under Part 61, a pilot can qualify in as few as 40 hours, but that's rare, and likely an unrealistic way to budget for flight training.

Aviation is an expensive pursuit, with the notable exception of unmanned aviation which is the most accessible type of aviation.

Requirements in the FAR/AIM

You can find a list of experience requirements for each certificate in the FAR/AIM. The FAR/AIM is two books combined into one: Federal Aviation Regulations and the Aeronautical Information Manual.

The FARs lists the experience requirements for pilot certificates and ratings as well as the rules pilots must follow.

The AIM has information that is not regulatory in nature but helpful for safe flight.

Most of your training will be done by a Certificated Flight Instructor (CFI). In a manned aircraft there will, usually, be two sets of controls so the CFI can show you what to do.

To be a pilot you must be able to read, speak, write, and understand the English language. English is the universal language in aviation, all pilots must speak English to fly internationally.

14 — **At 14 years** Can Fly a glider or hot-air balloon, take Part 107 exam (no priveliges till 16) C

16 — **At 16 years** Can solo an airplane, Earn Part 107 certificate & fly commercially

17 — **At 17 years** Can earn private pilot certificate

18 — **At 18 years** Can obtain Commercial Pilot Certificate

23 — **At 23 years** Can earn Airline Transport Pilot certificate.

ANY — **Any Age** Ground Study Simulated flights

FAQ:

•Can I be a pilot if I wear glasses or contact lenses?

Yes, you can fly with corrected vision.

•Do I need a medical to earn my Part 107?

No, you do not need a medical for Part 107.

•What if I have a medical condition that makes manned aviation unaccessible?

Not necessarily, you may still be eligible to be a remote pilot.

The FAA does not ennumerate a list of medical conditions that disqualify a candidate from flying unmanned aircraft.

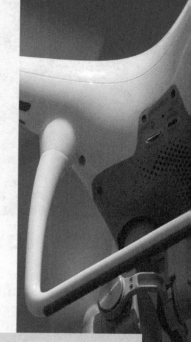

Most manned pilot certificates require you to hold an aviation medical certificate -- you get this after you pass a physical administered by an Aviation Medical Examiner. Part 67 in the FAR/AIM has the details. Part 107 does not require a medical.

Ready for the checkride?

How do you know if you are ready for the checkride? The FAA has documented the minimum standards of performance for pilots in the book Airman Certification Standards -- one exists for each certificate or rating.

Refer to this document to determine the level of proficiency you need to achieve. It us up to you and your flight instructor to make sure you are consistently reaching these minimum standards.

Once you have met all the requirements for the certificate and your CFI determines you have the proficiency to meet the standards of the ACS, you will get an endorsement to take the check ride. The endorsement is good for 60 days.

Logbooks are essential

Pilots keep track of their ground training time and flight time in a logbook. In most cases, you will need to show that you have done this training to be eligible for the FAA knowledge exam and the checkride.

Your CFI should teach you how to fill out your logbook and then you will both verify that you have the required experience to be eligible for the FAA knowledge exam and, if required, the check ride. The CFI will place these endorsements in your logbook, so be sure to bring it with you to the testing center and to the check ride.

Flight Experience

• To become a pilot you will need flight experience in the type of aircraft you want to fly for a living. For example, if you want to be a helicopter pilot flying an air ambulance service you should learn to fly helicopters. If you want a job at an airline like United, learn to fly airplanes. There are some pilots who learn to fly both, as this prepares them for more potential careers.

Fair warning: learning to fly is expensive. A private pilot certificate can cost upwards of $8,000 -- so many aspiring aviators look for a way to fund their flight raining -- one of those ways is to obtain a Commercial Remote Pilot certificate and make a business of flying the drone to pay for airplane lessons.

Other people become Ground Instructors, which is done by passing two FAA tests. The Fundamentals of Instructing, and an instructor knowledge exam. They can then teach ground school to other pilots to help them pass their knowledge tests.

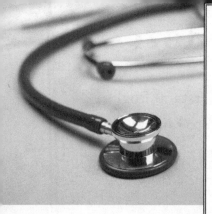

You do not need to take a medical exam to earn your Remote Pilot certificate.

Become a Remote Pilot: Fly a drone

Commercial drones can be as small as basketball and as large as a truck -- the size is dependent on the drone's function.

Drones are usually equipped with cameras or other scientific equipment to take observations.

Any industry that could benefit from surveillance or make use of aerial photography can use drones. They are quieter, more nimble, and less expensive than helicopters, and because they are considerably smaller, they can get into places helicopters are too large to fit.

Drones are used by the entertainment industry, law enforcement, real estate, city, federal and county governments, agriculture, landscaping, home repair, architecture, contractors — the list is almost endless. There is even a drone racing league.

To Earn your Part 107:

- Be at least 16 years old
- Be able to read, speak, write, and understand English
- Be in a physical and mental condition to safely fly a drone
- Pass the initial aeronautical knowledge exam: "Unmanned Aircraft General – Small (UAG)"

Knowledge test topic areas include:

- Applicable regulations relating to small unmanned aircraft system rating privileges, limitations, and flight operation
- Airspace classification and operating requirements, and flight restrictions affecting small unmanned aircraft operation
- Aviation weather sources and effects of weather on small unmanned aircraft performance
- Small unmanned aircraft loading and performance
- Emergency procedures
- Crew resource management
- Radio communication procedures
- Determining the performance of small unmanned aircraft
- Physiological effects of drugs and alcohol
- Aeronautical decision-making and judgment
- Airport operations
- Maintenance and preflight inspection procedures
- Operation at night

Study for the Exam

Did you know: Drones are the fastest growing segment of aviation in the United States?

Drone ground school can be done online at your own pace, or face to face with a a qualified ground instructor. 107 School is an online ground school for Part 107.

Once you complete ground school, you can take the sUAS knowledge test.

Learning to fly a drone

Learning to fly a drone by yourself is mostly trial and error. If you intend to fly in a park check with the park sponsors (like the city or county) to make sure it is allowed. Be cautious and respectful.

Your drone will have to be registered for commercial use and you will want to have a logbook to record your flights in. This will help document your experience.

Many professional drone operators have special cases to carry the aircraft in and addition cases for spare parts, maps, cameras, and a pocket for required documents such as contracts, permits, proof of insurance and the like.

Manned Pilots path to 107

If you already hold a U.S. pilot certificate issued under 14 CFR Part 61, you can obtain an sUAS certificate provided you have completed a flight review within the previous 24 months.

You will need to go to the FAA Safety Team (FAASTeam) website and complete the Part 107 Small UAS Initial (ALC-451 online training course.)

The topics area should be familiar as you learned these things for your private pilot certificate. In addition to weather and airspace, you'll be required to know about applicable regulations relating to sUAS, the privileges of the rating, limitations and flight operations including:

• Effects of weather on small unmanned aircraft performance
• Small unmanned aircraft loading and performance
• Emergency procedures
• Crew resource management
• Determining the performance of small unmanned aircraft
• Maintenance and preflight inspection procedures
• Operation at night

Then you'll need to log into your IACRA account and complete form 8710-13 FAA Airman Certificate and or Rating Applicant in IACRA. Follow the prompts and fill out the application, electronically sign it and submit for processing.

You will then have to make an appointment with an FAA Flight Standards District Office (FSDO), or an FAA Designated Pilot Examiner (DPE), or FAA Certificated Flight Instructor (CFI) so that they validate your identity.

Make sure to bring your government issued photo ID, your completed form 8710-13 and your online course completion certificate. After the review and sign your application you can expect to get your certificate in the mail.

Marketing yourself as a drone pilot

You may need to obtain a business license from your city or state to be a commercial drone pilot.

It is also likely flying the drone will be incidental to your job.

For example, if you work on a construction crew you may use your drone to inspect the roof.

If you want a job as a drone pilot you should make a demo reel sometimes referred to as a 'sizzle reel' showing your best work. Keep it about three minutes in length. If you add instrumental music to the reel (most people do) make sure you abide by copyright laws, you can license music from several websites that is royalty free.

Having a specialty or focus is key to landing new clients. People like to deal with contractors who are specialists, that do one particular task such as photogrammetry. Taking a particular type of photos like Real Estate or construction monitoring can be a good way to find work.

Skills drone pilots need

- Time management
- Organizational skills
- Basic marketing
- Attention to detail
- Video/Photo editing

It's like any other business, you're going to have to wear a whole lot of hats to get your business going if you are starting from scratch. You're going to be responsible for finding a need that you fulfill, presenting your solution to the market place, and asking for their business--all essential to market yourself.

Be a self starter and make sure you do good work in time people should notice.

If you're the boss and the employee, you need to make sure you spend your time productively. You have to be the drone pilot, the purchasing department, HR, vehicle maintenance, catering, handle dispatch, and if your work involves photos or video, you're the editing department as well.

There are countless tutorials and courses in the world that can teach the editing portion if you lack that ability now.

Industries that use drones

- Real Estate
- Television
- Law Enforcement
- Search & Rescue
- Geologists
- Hydrologists
- Landscapers
- City, State & County governments
- Industrial Construction
- Roofing
- Bridge Inspection
- Wildlife observation
- Entertainment/Media
- Athletic Trainers
- Architects
- Virtual tourism
- Countless other ideas

Drone Uses

• Real estate -- take the clients on a video tour of the property both outside and inside. First Person View (FPV) drones can be used for tour videos.

• Television -- great for aerial shots of sporting events, getting a bird's eye view of an area, following bike races to put the audience in the pack.

• Law enforcement -- some law enforcement agencies use drones to look for possibly armed suspects. It is a lot safer to send a drone into an unknown situation than it is to send a person. FPV drones have become popular for breaching an entry in close quarters combat.

• Search and Rescue -- a drone can search an area from the air much quicker than people can search on the ground.

• Geologist -- drones can get wide angle views of landslides and cliff faces without the wind and vibration created by helicopters that could potentially create a landslide.

Drone Uses

• Hydrologists -- drones can be used to follow streams, rivers and creeks to their point of termination to look for potential issues like illegal water diversion.

• Landscapers -- drones can be used to map property so the landscape architects can come up with design plans.

• City, State, and County governments--drones are used for aerial asset mapping -- like observing an outdoor storage facility to make sure all the assets such as bulldozers and street signs are still there. The can also be used for traffic studies.

• Industrial construction -- drones are used to inspect building's roofs and cornices several hundreds of feet in the air.

• Roofing -- drones are getting more popular for roof inspection.

• Bridge inspection -- it is easier to send a drone hundreds of feet into the air than it is to send a person.

Drone Uses

• Wildlife observation -- Drones are used to follow whales, observe ground animals and reptiles without putting a person in danger and tearing up sensitive land by hiking or driving in.

• Entertainment media -- drones can be used to video live events, or they can be the event -- there is a drone racing league.

• Athletic trainers -- a drone on the field can record plays made by the team which will be studied later.

• Architects -- architects use drones to get images or photogrammetry scans of a construction site area to best determine how to use the space.

• Virtual tourism -- with your drone you can go on hikes giving the viewer a first-person experience.

There are probably even more than haven't been thought of yet.

Flying Manned Aircraft

To get a certificate to fly a manned aircraft you will need to get a **student pilot certificate.**

You will need a CFI to help you fill out the online application the FAA Form 8710-13 on IACRA.

The CFI will need to be able to verify your physical place of residence (by looking at your driver's license) and after both you and the CFI electronically sign the application, it is submitted to the FAA.

You will be able to print out a temporary certificate, and in a few weeks your permanent student certificate which is plastic and has a hologram on it will be mailed to you..

You will need to have your Student Pilot Certificate available whenever you fly your aircraft.

Background Check

CFI Verification of citizenship

If you decide to study to fly manned aircraft, then your Flight Instructor will also need to verify your citizenship to give you your Transportation Security Administration endorsement.

If you are a U.S. citizen this is done by the CFI looking at your unexpired passport or birth certificate and verifying your citizenship. The CFI will then put an endorsement into your logbook verifying that they checked your citizenship.

If you are not a U.S. citizen, it is a little complicated. You will have to be fingerprinted by a third party and those finger prints submitted to the proper authorities. Most flight schools that train foreign nationals are well versed in this process and they can walk you through it.

Once you have the TSA endorsement, flight training can begin. There are multiple pilot certificates you can earn for manned aircraft: recreational pilot, sport pilot, private pilot, instrument pilot, commercial pilot, glider pilot, airship, seaplane, helicopter and airline transport pilot.

The FAA requires you to hold a student pilot certificate in order to fly solo — that's a few lessons away. Your CFI will decide when you have demonstrated proficiency to earn the chance to fly solo. You will also need an Aviation Medical Certificate before you solo.

While you can begin your flight training before obtaining a medical certificate, it's often best to get it early in your training, because if there is a medical condition that could possibly preclude you from obtaining a pilot certificate, it is best to find out sooner rather than later so you don't waste your money on flight training.

Medical Certificates

14 CFR 61.23 and 61.67 in the FARAIM have the details on the types of medical certificates available, their duration and the medical standards you are required to meet.

Most flight schools have a list of the local doctors that provide these pilot exams.

Side note:
There is a certificate known as the Sport Pilot certificate that does not require an aviation medial certificate.

Sport Pilots are allowed to fly two-place airplanes. As long as you hold a valid driver's license, you can be a Sport Pilot.

Professional Pilots

Professional pilots can fly for airlines, corporate, state agencies, the military, law enforcement, scientific research, air taxi and tourism.

While most of the jobs are for airplanes, flying a helicopter or airship is also an option.

In the civilian world, most all professional pilots began their career as private pilots. It is often called "a license to learn" because much of what a private pilot does is build their experience also known as their flight hours.

Every professional pilot was at one point a Private Pilot.

Private Pilot Eligibility

14 CFR 61.103 lists the eligibility requirements for private pilots. You can solo at age 16 but have to be
17 to earn your private pilot certificate.

You can do ground school before you begin your flight training, or during the process. Many people find that completing ground school first gives them a better understanding of what they are doing in the aircraft.

14 CFR 61.105 has a list topics you must know about such as Federal Aviation Regulations (FARs) that relate to private pilot privileges, limitations, and flight operations, accident reporting requirements of the National Transportation Safety Board, how to use the applicable portions of the Federal Aviation Regulations/Aeronautical Information Manual (FARAIM) and FAA advisory circulars, the use of special aviation maps called aeronautical charts, how to navigate landmark to landmark (this is called pilotage) dead reckoning, and navigation systems which are special instruments in the airplane.

Private Pilot Studies

You will also learn proper radio communication technique, weather theory and interpretation of forecasts and hazardous weather, safe and efficient operation of aircraft including collision avoidance, and recognition and avoidance of wake turbulence, aircraft performance, how to load the aircraft safely (this is known as weight and balance) principles of aerodynamics, power plants (that is a fancy word for engines) and aircraft systems, aerodynamics, emergency procedures, aeronautical decision making and physiology and how to plan flights.

You will need to pass the FAA private pilot knowledge test covering these topics with a score of at least 70 percent.

The material you learn for the private certificate is foundational, as it is also necessary for the recreation, sport, and Remote Pilot certificates.

Flight Training

•Training flights are usually done in two or four place single engine aircraft, one-on-one with a CFI.

•Flight lessons run about 60 to 90 minutes for local flights. There should a few minutes of briefing where the CFI tells what will be learned, then after the flight there will be a debriefed where you talk about what went well, what needs some work, and what the next lesson will be.

Pro-tip: Always use a syllabus, and study ahead to get the most out of the experience.

•Your flight experience will be a combination of dual lessons with the CFI and solo flight when you are alone in the aircraft.

• You will also fly what are known as cross country flights — flights with a straight-line distance of at least 50 nautical miles, and you will learn to fly in and out airports both with and without control towers. You will also log flights at night and by reference to the cockpit instruments only.

• To make the best progress you should fly at least two days a week.

How to begin your flight training

Most people begin their flight training with an introductory flight. You can make an appointment for this at the local flight school.

The discovery flight will begin with a flight instructor showing you how to use the checklist to do a pre-flight inspection of the aircraft. Aircraft have dual controls — a flight instructor will be sitting next to you or behind you and will guide you through the process.

The intro flight can be logged toward the 40 hours required for private pilot certificate.

Insist on using a syllabus and the Airman Certification Standards during training. Both provide the metrics as to the standards a pilot must fly. In order to be certified as a private pilot, you will need to reach these standards.

The Airmen Certification Standards (ACS) is available online from the FAA or can be purchased hard copy at most pilot supply stores. The ACS lists the knowledge required of private pilots along with the tasks you must do and flight maneuvers you will need to perform to be a pilot.

Pay special attention to the metrics give for aircraft performance, for exam "maintain altitude within 100 feet and heading +/- 10 degrees" because these are the minimum standards you will be tested — like getting a "C" in school.

Strive for excellence

You will be flying with people you care about, so do your best to do better the minimum standard, for example strive to maintain altitude within 20 feet and heading within 5 degrees.

You will demonstrate these things to a Designated Pilot Examiner (DPE) during a practical flight test known as a check ride. The DPE will be the person to issue you the pilot certificate.

Pro-Tip: *Fly at least twice a week, but no more than three days a week. You will need time between lessons to process the information you learned.*

Insist the CFI use and follow a syllabus. A syllabus lists the tasks you will learn and the knowledge you will need to know and the order in which it will be presented.

You will get the most out of your training if you read ahead in the syllabus and study the material prior to the flight lesson.

Jobs for Private Pilots

For most aviation jobs you will need to hold at least a commercial pilot certificate, however there are a few a private pilot can do, such as working as a glider tow pilot or as a demo pilot for aircraft sales.

To tow gliders a private pilot who has logged at least 100 hours as pilot in command and receives ground and flight training in gliders. This can be a fun summer job and you build your time quickly.

As a demo pilot for aircraft sales you would be flying with potential customers who are interested in buy the airplane. This job can involve a lot of travel and you build your cross country time quickly.

Skills a Private Pilot should have
- Good time management skills
- Good study habits
- Self-discipline
- Ability to learn

The Instrument rating

After completing of the Private Pilot certificate many pilots pursue an instrument rating. This rating allows you to legally fly in clouds.

During your Private Pilot training you will receive three hours of instrument training as sort of an emergency procedure, as an instrument pilot you will build on these skills.

As flight instructor, charter pilot or airline pilot most of your flying will done on instrument flight plans, so an instrument rating and solid IFR skills are a must.

To be eligible for the rating, you must have logged at least 50 hours of cross-country flight time as pilot in command. At least 10 of these hours must be in airplanes for an instrument-airplane rating.

You will need to have logged at least 40 hours of actual or simulated instrument time on the areas of operation listed in FAR 61.65(c). Some of this time can be logged in a FAA approved Advanced Aviation Training Device, commonly known as a simulator.

At least 15 hours of this training must be from an authorized instructor in the aircraft category for the instrument rating sought.

Under Part 141 the 50 hours of cross-country flight is waived, but if you intend to be a professional pilot you will want to get all the cross country time and instrument time you can, because that's the kind of flying your future employers will want to see.

Skills an Instrument Pilot should have
- The ability to multi task
- Good study habits
- Self-discipline
- Ability to learn
- Attention to detail

Pro-tip: The FARs allow you to do approximately half of the required 40 hours in the FAA approved Advanced Aviation Training Device. They are usually less expensive than an airplane or helicopter and make a better learning environment because when things get difficult, the Instructor can hit the pause button and you can discuss the challenge you are facing. Try that in an airplane.

Required skills for Commercial pilots

- Good time management skills

- Good study habits

- Self-discipline

- Good communication skills

- Ability to learn

- Good customer service skills

Commercial Pilot Certificate

To have a career as a professional pilot you will need to hold a commercial pilot certificate. A commercial pilot certificate allows you to work for someone else. If you want to be in business for yourself in addition to a commercial certificate you will need to get a business license and FAA approval for your business.

To obtain a Commercial certificate you must have logged at least 190 hours of flight experience if you train under an accredited Part 141 school, or 250 hours if you train under Part 61.

Just like with the private pilot certificate, you must receive the necessary training, documented in your logbook or official training records, to pass the FAA knowledge and practical flight examinations.

You must be at least 18 years of age and hold an FAA Second-Class Medical certificate to work as a Commercial pilot.

While it is possible to obtain a commercial pilot certificate without an instrument rating, it is limiting.

For example, you will not be able to fly paying customers farther than 50 nautical miles from the point of departure and you will not be allowed to fly passengers at night.

You can earn a commercial pilot certificate for airplane single engine land or multiengine land, and for single or multiengine sea if you want to fly a seaplanes.

Building hours with a commercial certificate

Every aviation job requires a certain amount of experience, that is flight hours logged. There are a variety of jobs you can do as a relatively low-time pilot with a commercial certificate.

• **Skydive pilot:** Your job is to take the skydivers up to altitude where they will jump out of your perfectly good airplane.

• **Pipeline and power line patrol pilot.** This requires you to fly fairly low and slow as you verify the pipe or the power lines are intact.

• **Agricultural pilot.** These jobs include crop dusting or aerial reseeding such as after a forest fire. There are flight schools that offer specific training for this career position.

• **Aerial survey pilot:** In a specially equipped airplane you will fly a pre established pattern to map an area.

• **Air ambulance jobs:** You could be the copilot on an air ambulance flight carrying the injured and sick to life saving medical treatment.

• **Banner tow pilot:** these are popular jobs along coastlines, resort areas and over sports stadiums. The aircraft you fly will be equipped with a special hook and you will be trained to pick and drop the banner at the appropriate time. You will be flying for several hours at a time at a specific altitude and a specific airspeed to keep the banner readable for people on the ground.

More ways to build experience

• **Charter pilot**: When you reach a certain level of experience found under Part 135 in the FARAIM, you will be eligible to fly as a charter pilot. Your job will be to get paying passengers safely from Point A to Point B as comfortably and economically as possible.

• **Flight instructor.** You will learn how to teach other people to fly. It is a quick way to build experience for other flying jobs, and it can be some the most rewarding flying you will do in your career and it is your chance to share your love of aviation.

A note about flight instructing: you will be the first point of contact for many aspiring pilots, so do your best to make it a positive experience for them. If you don't like being a teacher, find another way to build your hours. There are some people who love flight instructing so much and who are good enough to make a career out of it. These instructors are often in high demand.

Fly for an agency

• Fish and Game, Forest Service, Law Enforcement

While these are not time building jobs, they can be very fulfilling because you are making a positive difference in your community and be part of a team.

• Specialized Commercial work -- air tours

Air tours are a popular way to building experience. These jobs are often seasonal. You may work from May to October taking tourists around the local sights. It helps if you are naturally comfortable talking to people. These tours are done by floatplanes, helicopters, airplanes and even airships.

Consider this:

If you are of smaller stature you may find it easier to get a job as a skydive pilot, tour or ambulance pilot especially in helicopters because the smaller the pilot, the more useful load (baggage, fuel and passengers) can be put on board. **48**

Airline Transport Pilot

• You will need at least 1,500 hours of flight time if you do your training under part 61 or 1250 hours if you train at an accredited Part 141 program to qualify for the Airline Transport Pilot certificate.

This certificate, like the others involves specific ground knowledge, passing an FAA knowledge test and a practical test. Many airlines hire applicants who meet ATP minimums, as they have the hours and experience, and the knowledge test completed and they will do the practical test as part of their airline training.

• Airline pilots and corporate pilots and professional pilots with state and local agencies are often required to hold an ATP certificate.

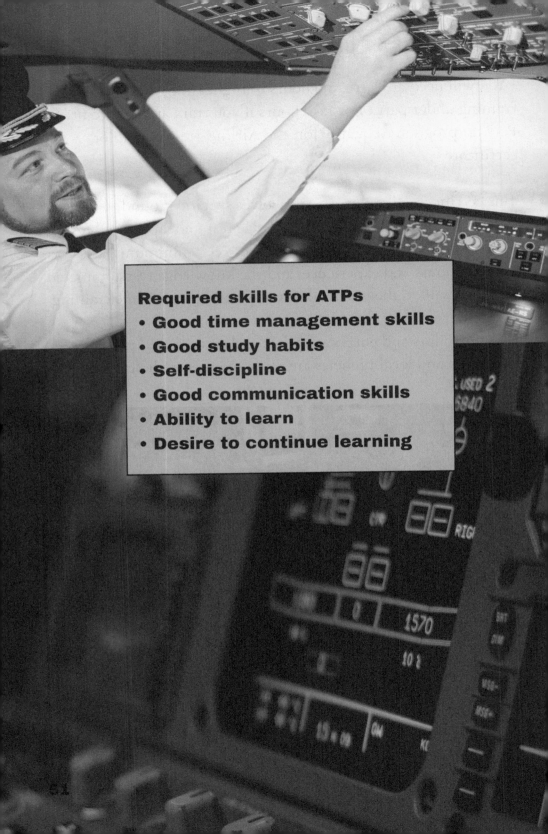

Required skills for ATPs
- **Good time management skills**
- **Good study habits**
- **Self-discipline**
- **Good communication skills**
- **Ability to learn**
- **Desire to continue learning**

ATP

Pro-tip: Airline hiring is cyclical -- sometimes there is a shortage of qualified applicants, other times there is a glut.

In addition to having at least 1,500 hours of flight experience and an ATP rating, some airlines require their applicants have at least a two-year college degree, some want a four-year, others don't require a degree but strongly encourage their pilots to pursue higher education.

The college degree, if required, need not be in aviation, in fact it is often a good idea to pursue a degree in something besides aviation in the event that you decided being an airline pilot isn't for you.

Many pilots have degrees in business, marketing, or finance because these skills can be used in many jobs.

More Aviation Careers

Designated Pilot Examiner

A Designated Pilot Examiner is a person who give check rides to people seeking pilot certificates and ratings. To be a DPE you need to be flight instructor first, and usually you will need several years of experience.

DPEs are selected by the FAA and are trained to administer the flight tests, also known as check rides. Most DPEs begin by providing private pilot exams and as their experience increases they can apply to administer other tests.

Required skills:
- Good Communication skills
- Good organization skills
- Ability to control temper

Other Aviation jobs that don't require a pilot certificate

Line crew

Line crew sometimes called line boys although both men and women work the job are the people who refuel airplanes at general aviation airports.

It is a very physical job so you should be prepared to climb ladders, haul hoses and handle customer's baggage. It helps if you have some mechanical aptitude and know how to drive a 5-speed truck, a golf cart and or a forklift.

While line crew don't get paid very much especially at smaller businesses, they do make valuable business contacts. That owner of that KingAir you refueled might help you land a better job someday.

Required skills:
• Good communication skills
• Physical Fitness
• Cheerful attitude
• A good memory
• Ability to learn

Flight School Dispatcher

Flight school dispatch person
Like a receptionist, but the best ones have a working knowledge of aviation -- often you can arrange to get a few hours of flight training here and there. The dispatch person through software keeps track of the schedule ing of the fleet including when the aircraft are due to routine maintenance.

You need to have good listening skills and pay attention to details to be a dispatcher -- if a customer says they don't fit in a particular airplane because they are too tall, make a note of that in their file.

Make sure to read the notes in these files because there is no quicker way to lose a customer than to put them in an airplane they don't fit in because you didn't read the notes.

Required skills:
- Good Communication Skills
- A cheerful attitude
- A good memory
- The ability to multitask

Air Traffic Control

To be an Air Traffic Controller you will need at least a two year degree from an accredited school.

Most of these schools require the ATC students to take private, instrument and commercial ground school. The college degree may require you have at least a private pilot certificate.

Once you apply your application will be placed in a pool and if selected by the FAA, you will go to Oklahoma city for training. You must be hired before your 30th birthday, because the FAA intends for you to have a career of at least 20 years.

You may work in a small tower at a regional airport and when you get more experience you can apply for work at larger faculties where you will make more money.

Required skills
- Ability to learn quickly
- Good spatial skills
- Good communication skills
- Good stress management

Airline Dispatcher

Dispatchers at the airline level do the flight planning for aircraft on specific routes. Many colleges and universities have degrees that incorporate courses to become dispatchers and you will have to take and pass an FAA knowledge test for Dispatchers.

Required skills
- Ability to learn quickly
- Good communication skills
- Good organization skills
- Good math skills

Mechanic, A&P

To become an aviation mechanic you can attend a program at a tech college (they are usually 18 to 24 months) or work at an FBO as a maintenance assistant and obtain on the job training. Either way you will have to take and pass a knowledge test and demonstrate practical skills to become an Airframe and Powerplant mechanic.

Real world note: mechanics are always in demand, and not just in the aviation industry. It is not uncommon for automobile and aircraft manufacturers to recruit at tech colleges in search of talent.

Airframe and Power Plant (A&P) is how most people begin their careers. After a few years and a few hundred hours of experience you can apply to obtain Inspection Authority (IA) which means you can inspect the work of others and sign it off.

If you are working at a flight school and you hold at least a private pilot certificate in addition to a mechanic certificate you become extra valuable to an employer because you can potentiality ferry airplanes and test flying after maintenance.

Pro-tip: many A&Ps pursue pilot certificates because it makes them more valuable to employers.

Military pilot

Being a pilot in the United States military can be a very rewarding career -- it is also one of the more challenging ones to get. You have to be in good physical condition and of good moral character and be committed to the military life. The requirements to be a military pilot can vary from branch to branch -- and they change when the needs of the military change. Most military pilots have a college degree or are working on a college degree. The service commitment for military pilots is often seven years or more. You are encouraged to add to your academic credentials as well as flying skills.

Experience as a military pilot can help you qualify for a job in the space program, to pilot Air Force One, various law enforcement flying jobs, and of course the airlines.

Required skills
• Good communication skills
• Physical fitness
• A positive attitude
• A good memory
• Ability to learn quickly

Federal Aviation Administration

The FAA has many different jobs. You can find them listed at USAJobs.gov. You could become an Aviation Safety Inspector for general aviation or the airlines, a computer analyst, a public relations officer, the lists are endless. Most of the jobs require some college, and often employees are encouraged to add advanced degrees.

Required skills
• Ability to learn
• Good communication skills
• Good organization skills
• Good at office politics

National Transportation Safety Board Accident Investigator

When there has been an accident involving transportation be it on the ground, sea, rail or air, the NTSB investigates. Their job is to make transportation safer. While you do not necessarily have to be a pilot to work at the NTSB, it can make you more competitive. A college degree is also helpful in an aviation related discipline such as Human Factors.

Required skills
• Ability to learn quickly
• Good communication skills
• Good organization skills
• Good observation skills

Airport Manager

An airport manager's primary responsibility is to ensure that the airport operates efficiently and safely. You will be managing staff, overseeing building and infrastructure maintenance and ensuring the airport is in compliance with FAA safety standards.

You need to be a good communicator as you will be the go-between with airport tenants and the airport sponsors such as the city or country, as well as the FAA.

To be an airport manager, you will likely need an undergraduate degree in aviation or a related field, as well as several years of experience in airport operations. Many airport managers begin their careers as maintenance workers or operations technicians at an airport where they learn the job and get practical experience before they move into management roles. Many airport managers seek degrees in business administration or public administration.

Required skills
- Good time management skills
- Good leadership skills
- Good budgeting skills
- Ability to learn
- Good communication skills
- Good organization skills
- Good math skills

Aviation Museum Curator

Museum curators make decisions about what content should be shared in a museum and when.
Aviation Museum curators tend to be very passionate about aviation and this shows in their work.

Museum curators often design, install and arrange installations in museums. They create budgets for artifact acquisition and restoration and help plan special events such as lectures and other activities centered on the exhibits, for example "Vintage Biplane day" when they invite local pilots with vintage biplanes to visit the museum and have pilots give talks about their airplanes.

Most Museum Curators have a master's degree or higher, often a Master of Fire Arts.

Required skills:
• Ability to manage people
• Leadership skills
• Communication skills
• The ability to research potential exhibits
• The ability to network

107 School offers a complete course to help you pass
your Part 107 knowledge exam and become a safe remote
pilot. Our course includes reading, watching about 140
short videos, and taking quizzes and exams to reinforce
what you learn. You will pass your test, or your money
back.

Earning your 107:
Supplemental Information
by John Ellis, AGI

The following pages are all about Part 107 the rules that apply to apply to commercial civil unmanned flight operations in the US. These pages are an expansion on the information already provided to give an introduction to the process of earning your Part 107 certificate to fly drones commercially in the USA.

What is Part 107? Do I need a Part 107?

Are you interested in drones?
Want to fly them
to help your business?

What is Part 107? Does everyone need one to fly a drone?

The short answer is no, not everyone who wants to fly a drone needs a part 107 certificate, unless they intend on using that drone in the furtherance of a business.

Part 107 refers to 14 CFR Part 107 Small Unmanned Aircraft Systems, the part of the
Code of Federal Regulations that pertains to the flight of civil unmanned aircraft between .55 and 55 pounds flown in the United States for commercial purposes.

To be eligible to earn your part 107 certificate with a small unmanned aircraft system rating, a person must be at least 16 years of age, be able to read, speak, write and understand the English language, and not know or have reason to know that they have a physical or mental illness that would interfere with the safe opeartion of an sUAS.

Recreational Drone Pilots take TRUST

Recreational Flyers need to take the The Recreational UAS Safety Test (TRUST), and can never earn any money flying their drones unless they decide to become part 107 operators in the future. They can only fly for fun and recreation.

The big difference is commercial interest. Of course, 107 Pilots can fly for fun and recreation. Recreational pilots can never fly for money, or to help a business. The FAA fines those who ignore these rules.

Eligibility to Earn Part 107:

• Be at least 16 years old
• Be able to read, speak, write, and understand English
• Be in a physical and mental condition to safely fly a drone
• Pass the initial aeronautical knowledge exam: "Unmanned Aircraft General – Small (UAG)"

Knowledge test topic areas include:

• Applicable regulations relating to small unmanned aircraft system rating privileges, limitations, and flight operation
• Airspace classification and operating requirements, and flight restrictions affecting small unmanned aircraft operation
• Aviation weather sources and effects of weather on small unmanned aircraft performance
• Small unmanned aircraft loading and performance
• Emergency procedures
• Crew resource management
• Radio communication procedures
• Determining the performance of small unmanned aircraft
• Physiological effects of drugs and alcohol
• Aeronautical decision-making and judgment
• Airport operations
• Maintenance and preflight inspection procedures
• Operation at night, night illusions, & eye physiology
• Operations over people & moving vehicles

Study for the Exam

Drone ground school can be done online at 107 School, we have a complete online ground school for Part 107 and cover all of these topics thoroughly.

107 School covers all of this material, and teaches you everything you need to know to operate professionally as a certified commercial drone pilot in our easy to use course. We have broken the material down into brief topics covered in short form videos that average around three minutes in length.

You can watch all of our videos, and take our quizzes and exams online, or you can use our mobile apps for iTunes or Android to take our course anywhere you choose. Our course will take about two weeks if you study one hour a day, and after that period you will know part 107 really well.

Once you complete ground school, you can take the sUAS knowledge test, which is administered by PSI Testing and costs $175 to take. We guarantee you'll pass or your money back*.

Manned Pilot's Path to a Part 107

If you are a manned pilot with a certificate issued under Part 61, and have completed a flight review in the previous 24 months, you have a different path to your Part 107.

Manned pilots just need to take a brief educational course online to earn their part 107 certificate because they have already demonstrated knowledge of most of the material covered on the Part 107 exam by taking their Private Pilot knowledge exam.

It's this material overlap that makes earning a Part 107 so desirable, you'll have a heads up on the material you'll need for your Private Pilot certificate, and the process will be much easier for you.

Manned Pilots need to go to the FAA Safety Team (FAASTeam) website and enroll in and pass an FAA couse titled ALC-451: Part 107 Small Unmanned Aircraft Systems, since they already understand airspace, and many regulations, and need to learn a smaller amount of new information.

The course for Part 61 Manned Pilots is online at: www. faasafety.gov

The FAA also has a useful FAQ page: https://www.faa.gov/faq?combine=&field_faq_category_target_id=1491

Subjects in the course:

The topics for the test should be familiar as most of it is covered during private pilot ground training. In addition to weather and airspace, they'll be required to know about applicable regulations relating to sUAS, the privileges of the rating, limitations and flight operations including:

• Effects of weather on small unmanned aircraft performance
• Small unmanned aircraft loading and performance
• Emergency procedures
• Crew resource management
• Determining the performance of small unmanned aircraft
• Maintenance and preflight inspection procedures
• Operation at night, night illusions, eye physiology
• Operations over people and the 4 categories of drones
• Operations over moving vehicles

Then they'll need to log into their IACRA account and complete form 8710-13 FAA Airman Certificate and or Rating Applicant in IACRA. Follow the prompts and fill out the application, electronically sign it and submit for processing.

Manned pilots will then have to make an appointment with an FAA Flight Standards District Office (FSDO), or an FAA Designated Pilot Examiner (DPE), or FAA Certificated Flight Instructor (CFI) so that they validate their identity.

They must bring their government issued photo ID, their completed form 8710-13 and their online course completion certificate. Afterwards they get their certificate in the mail.

I'm Not a Manned Pilot, How do I get a 107?

So what about all of us who are not manned pilots? What do we have to do to become a remote pilot?

We've already said that to be eligible to earn your part 107 certificate with a small unmanned aircraft system rating, a person must be at least 16 years of age, be able to read, speak, write and understand the English language, be in physical and mental condition to safely fly a drone, and pass the knowledge exam.

Interestingly, you can pass you exam before you turn 16, and then apply for your remote pilot certificate when you turn 16, so you can pass the exam at age 14, and the company that offers the test allows registrants to be 14.

Even if you are just promoting your business with a video from your drone, that is in furtherance of a business. A realtor that takes a photo for a listing without a part 107 could get serious fines that far exceed the cost of earning the certificate, or many months worth of sales commissions.

To earn your certificate, you are going to need to pass a knowledge exam of 60 questions with a score of 70% or higher. The exam costs $175 to take, and covers the knowledge you'll need to fly remotely piloted aircraft in the national airspace.

107 School teaches all of this material, and simulates the FAA questions so that you are prepared to succeed on the actual exam. We guarantee that if you complete all of our course, you'll pass the exam.

You'll also have a good foundation to be a safe real world 107 operator, so that you can be confident to not cause yourself unneccessary grief.

Is the test hard?

The test covers a significant amount of material. It does take training and effort to learn everything you are going to need to know in order to be successful on the knowledge exam. So, it is challenging but easy enough to pass with enough training.

As a ground instructor, the material contains a significant amount of private pilot level training, and a good amount of unmanned aviation specific rules that are not covered in the private pilot level courses. You need to know the airspace system and how it will affect where and how high you can fly.

As drones do not have any persons on board, they do not have right of way, and you must know how to stay out of the way of manned aviation. This is why the FAA takes violations so seriously. They can't always monitor every inch of airspace all the time, but the believe by puishing bad actors severely that they can keep the skies safer.

With our course, you will need to spend at least 15-20 hours studying in order to succeed. There are about 8 hours of videos to watch, and you may rewatch a few to make sure the information is being retained.

We recommend an hour a day of study for a two week period, and add supplemental study if you'd like. To complete the course, we want to see you score higher than you will need to do so on your FAA knowledge exam, just to make sure your success isn't in doubt.

To earn your 107, you must pass the knowledge exam

Our course has over 140 videos that average just over three minutes in length, and an extensive question bank that is correlated to our videos. If you spend around an hour or two a day with our content, and study with good effort, you will complete the course in a couple of weeks and be thoroughly prepared for your exam.

Our course was written by an AGI, an Advanced Ground Instructor, certified by the FAA as qualified to teach ground school to manned aviation candidates seeking private, sport, or commercial pilot certificates. To earn the AGI certificate, applicants must pass two difficult knowledge exams that demonstrate instructor level knowledge.

Our chief instructor also produced the very first video course to teach part 107 knowledge exam prep material. He sat for his Part 107 knowledge exam in 2016, becoming one of the very first FAA certified commercial drone pilots under part 107.

Carry your certificate with you for all missions

Your Certificate has no photo

Once you earn your Remote Pilot certificate you will likely carry it like most do, in your wallet with your Photo ID.

If you are questioned by Law Enforcement you are to provide proof of your status as a remote pilot, and either your Driver's license or some other photographic proof of identification.

Requirements for Remote Pilot Certificate:

• Must be easily accessible by the remote pilot during all UAS operations

• Certificate holders must complete an online recurrent training every
24 calendar months to maintain aeronautical knowledge recency

• Must keep print out of certificate of completion of recurrent training
along with sUAS Registration during UAS operations.

Once we have earned our certificate we need to have it with us during all UAS operations, and we have to complete an online recurrent training course every 24 calendar months to maintain our aeronautical knowledge.

It's a course that only takes a couple of hours to complete and can be done anywhere you have internet access. Once you complete that course, you print out your certificate of completion and have to carry that as well.

Take the test

Once you are prepared to pass the exam you will need to take your
knowledge exam. To do that use the following steps from the FAA, the test is currently offered by PSI Testing.

The test us caked the Unmanned Aircraft-General exam (UAG), and you have to take it at a PSI testing center. This 60 question multiple-choice test requires that you answer 70% correct or higher to pass.

Once you pass, you will be issued a temporary certificate and be allowed to fly as a remote PIC.

After you've had your certificate for two years, you will need to take recurrent training to continue to use your remote pilot privileges.

The FAA does its recurrent training online via recurrent course ALC-677 for part 107 pilots.

You must print out your certificate after passing your recurrent course online, don't worry, this will be two years after your initial certificate is issued, the intent is to keep remote pilots informed of any updates or changes in the laws.

Certificate
of Achievement

This is to certify that

FAA
Aviation Safety

has successfully completed the
FAA Safety Team Aviation Learning Center Online
Course

Part 107 Small Uas Recurrent

Course Number ALC-677
Presented by FAASTeam

Certificate Number

Patricia Mathes

Patricia Mathes, Manager, National FAA Safety Team

Example recurrent certificate

Dealing with the FAA is straightforward, but they are a governmental bureacracy and you have to realize they have a way for doing everything, and you have to do things their way.

Our course details all of the steps along the path toward earning your certificate, but we wanted to use this ebook as a introduction to our future students, and wanted to detail all of the steps to completing your paperwork for your certificate.

Steps to Become a Certificated Commercial Drone Pilot:

Step 1: Obtain an FAA Tracking Number (FTN) by creating an Integrated Airman Certification and Rating Application (IACRA) profile prior to registering for a knowledge test. Make sure you record both your FTN and IACRA information somewhere safe.

Step 2: Schedule an appointment with a FAA-approved Knowledge Testing Center. Be sure to bring a government-issued photo ID to your test.

Step 3: Pass the initial aeronautical knowledge test: "Unmanned Aircraft General – Small (UAG)". Knowledge test.

Step 4: Complete FAA Form 8710-13 for a remote pilot certificate

(FAA Airman Certificate and/or Rating Application) using the electronic FAA Integrated Airman Certificate and/or Rating Application system (IACRA)*

1. Login with username and password
2. Click on "Start New Application" and A) Application Type "Pilot", B) Certifications "Remote Pilot", C) Other Path Information, D) Start Application
3. Follow application prompts

Step 5: A confirmation email will be sent when an applicant has completed the TSA security background check. This email will provide instructions for printing a copy of the temporary remote pilot certificate from IACRA.

Step 6: A permanent remote pilot certificate will be sent via mail once all other FAA-internal processing is complete.

Step 7: Have your Remote Pilot Certificate available whenever you fly

Keep Your Remote Pilot Certificate Current

It is important for all pilots, including Certified Remote Pilots, to keep their aviation knowledge up to date. If you have a Remote Pilot Certificate, you are required to have completed one of the following online training courses within the previous 24 calendar months to operate UAS under part 107:

Anyone who holds a part 107 remote pilot certificate (regardless of aeronautical knowledge recency):

• Complete the Part 107 Small UAS Recurrent (ALC-677) online training course (no cost)

Manned pilots who take the alternate route will also take a different recurrent training course every two years. Part 107 remote pilots who are also certificated with a current flight review under part 61:

• Complete the Part 107 Small UAS Recurrent (ALC-515) online training course (no cost)

Airman Knowledge Testing Supplement for Sport Pilot, Recreational Pilot, Remote Pilot, and Private Pilot

Current as of
2020

U.S. Department
of Transportation

Federal Aviation
Administration

DO NOT MARK IN THIS BOOK

Pro-tip: buy a physical copy of the Airman Kowledge Testing Supplement (FAA-CT-8080)

All of the questions on the FAA knowledge exam that utilizes figures has to use the images contained in this publication. This is why we use the same images in our FAA style questions.

This publication is given to you during your FAA knowledge exam for you to
reference while taking the exam.

Having a physical copy with you while you study will help prepare you for the actual exam, and allow you interact with the material by engaging more senses, which helps you retain the knowledge. All of our test questions that reference these images have a copy of the image downloaded from this publication, but if you are using a phone, the images are very small and having a printed copy is very helpful.

Spend time with our course on a daily basis for a few weeks. About an hour a day of studying should give you enough exposure to this material to really understand it, if you need more time daily, that's fine, understand your needs as a learner and adapt our materials to help you study.